SINGLE SERVING
FOR SINGLE WOMEN:
A FIFTY DAY DEVOTIONAL

SINGLE SERVING FOR SINGLE WOMEN: A FIFTY DAY DEVOTIONAL

Tamara B. Gibbs

ISBN: 1530870712
ISBN 13: 9781530870714
Library of Congress Control Number: 2016905758
CreateSpace Independent Publishing Platform
North Charleston, South Carolina

For every girl who has ever had to buy her own birthday dinner, cake, card, and flowers.
For every woman courageously celebrating herself.
For Mamacita, a compassionate teacher of self-love.
For Rashad, who taught me maturity and wisdom.

Contents

Hope Along the Journey

Introduction

A SINGLE SERVING

The demitasse spoon is smaller than a teaspoon. It serves up a delicate portion. Isn't this how God handles us? He lovingly and gently doles out  doses of wisdom. He seldom gives us super-sized portions. He knows this would overwhelm us. Instead, our growth in relationship with Him and others, as well as the development of our self-awareness, takes precious time. It can evolve over months—even years. For the single woman, it has the potential to become a deep, abiding love for the woman in the mirror. Some people are never afforded this opportunity as they juggle the responsibilities and distractions that come with career, children, and spouses. However, let's not forget that there are also women living *single* within the covenant of marriage. Whatever the circumstance, selfishly and beautifully, the single woman can consciously and willingly carve out time to nurture and improve the inner woman. The process is both a blessing and a curse. It can be liberating, peaceful, fulfilling, and, well, downright lonely.

That tension between joy and frustration is a tightrope of faith. There's the thrill of adventure as she strikes out on her own, brazenly dining alone at a restaurant or climbing Machu Picchu. Perhaps after great disappointment, she lets bitterness take root and builds a solid fortress around her heart or she wears her heart on her sleeve—or, better yet, in her hand—giving it away without regard for greater discernment. I've bought lessons on either end of the spectrum, and I've paid dearly for my choices. I've also learned a great deal about life, love, and leaning on my Abba Father.

This devotional journey is meant to be your companion. Tuck it under your arm, toss it in your bag, or lend it to another single soul. It's divided into three sections inspired by that familiar scripture in Chapter 13 of the Book of Corinthians: faith, hope, and love. They're the tenets of the Christian faith, and, for the purpose of this book, they're the labels for each leg of the single woman's race toward personal victory. At any given time, she may find herself happily serving the Lord, a graceful lady in waiting. She may battle with temptation and envy. She may need to renew her hope after great disappointment and loss. Ultimately, she should discover herself through the incomparable power of the Great Love.

It is comforting to serve a God who wastes nothing. Not one experience—good or bad—is in vain. Not one tear or celebration is without purpose. Everything the single woman experiences on her journey is recycled, fashioned into something that is ultimately for her good. Her years without consistent companionship mean just as much as the moment she may walk down the aisle. It is all small doses of His love—even when it doesn't feel like enough.

It's OK

It's OK. Really, it is. I promise.

I'm writing this as a single and childless woman who has spent a lifetime wishing on stars, singing (sometimes howling) at the moon, and fervently praying for a family of my own.

Then one day it occurred to me that this thorn, like the one that Paul spoke of in his letter to Corinth, was for a reason. God was using all that disappointment, all that heartbreak, and all that long suffering in this area of my life to serve a purpose.

Unlike most books with a similar theme, I'm not going to claim you can just pray it away. I'm not going to tell you that your Boaz is coming. I'm not going to tell you that if you speak it into existence, it will come. All those things may very well be true. There's also a chance that they might not be God's plan for your life. The honest truth is, we don't know.

And it's OK.

After many trials and triumphs, I'm getting to a place where God is my portion. Getting there wasn't easy. Staying there was twice as hard. You must remind yourself daily. A single serving every day.

So I encourage you to find peace and to see the grace in your circumstance. Develop a personal relationship with the Lord as you take one step at a time on your journey. Fully understand that your Holy Father is all you need to get by. In seasons of lack, He is a bare necessity.

Know the fullness of joy even in the absence of your heart's desire. Recognize the grace and favor that still exists in your singleness and perhaps childlessness. Shout, "Hallelujah!" Declare your love for your Heavenly Father, even when things aren't happening fast enough or in the way you'd hoped and planned.

1

This devotional is a daily single serving of hope and encouragement. After all, you are a single woman serving and delighting in Him. These pages are reminders to be so hidden in Him, in service to Him, and laboring for Him that you begin to experience peace that surpasses all understanding. This journey to wisdom and contentment is not easy. But I'm willing, if you are.

"The Lord is my Shepherd. I shall not want."

PSALM *23:1*

SINGLE SERVING

Are you OK with being single? Why or why not? Be honest.

Love* (with an asterisk)

Webster's Dictionary defines an asterisk (*) as "a symbol that is used in printed text especially to tell someone to read a note that can be found at the bottom of a page." It signals to the reader that there's a tidbit more information than what was initially provided at first glance. Sometimes the quest for love (or what at first appears to be love) can work in the same way. Some suitors may have footnotes or disclaimers attached to their promises of friendship, relationship, or even covenant. This should not discourage the search for true love. A single woman should always remain open to finding a soul mate. She has every right to pray for a Boaz, a Lapidoth, an Aquila, or a Psalm 15 man:

> **[He] who keeps an oath even when it hurts, and does not change their mind.**
>
> **PSALM 15:4**

Now that's honorable, dependable, and true. That's Johnny-and-June-walk-the-line kind of love. Can we agree that's worth singing about and waiting for? But as seasons of singleness follow one after the other, settling for something that's not even remotely close to that is tempting. At least you can finally RSVP with a plus one, right? At least, you have someone to hang out with. Here's where a single woman must not only know her worth, but also treat it like a 401(k) and invest in its growth. No, she should not foolishly hold out for perfection (it doesn't exist). Instead, her time is better spent waiting for real.

Real *chivalry.*
Real *reciprocity.*
Real *courage.*

Real *faith.*

Real *love.*

Love not only opens doors and shields you from traffic, but behind closed doors (when no one else is watching), it handles you with care and respect. Love not only gives; it also takes mutual sacrifice. Love not only asks us to be brave; it also asks us to be vulnerable. Love not only believes in the unseen; it makes the unseen possible. Notice that there are no asterisks denoting an unhealed past, narcissism, selfishness, insecurity, immaturity, pride, or fear. So no more settling for love with an asterisk. You deserve God's best. Period.

~~~

*"Husbands, love your wives, as Christ loved the church
and gave himself up for her..."*

EPHESIANS 5:25

~~~

SINGLE SERVING

Consider God's best for you. What qualities might a potential spouse possess?

Nobody's Coming

As the caregiver for her chronically ill grandmother, my mother had poured out her last ounce of energy. The fatigue was in her face as she grew increasingly weary and frustrated at what she felt was a lack of support from others. I gently but firmly told her, "Nobody's coming." Years later, it's a phrase we use to remind us that sometimes there is no rescue or immediate relief from trials. Sometimes we are called to go it alone.

They say that a child idealizes the absent parent. I think the same can be said for the single person waiting to find love. There are days when your lack is palpable, emotionally heavy. There are tough, tough days when it's just you. The silence is not only deafening but just plain lonely. A hard day at work gets no listening ear. There's no shoulder for a teary eye, no hand or strong arm for the weary soul to embrace.

Consider the one source who has loved you unconditionally your entire life. For some, it may be a parent or a sibling, or perhaps a pet. Conjure the purest emotion of unconditional love, a feeling that, come what may, this entity that the Lord planned for you while He formed you in your mother's womb will never cease loving you.

After meditating on that for a while, you begin to understand it was Him all along. It was God manifesting himself in a way that you could always recognize and receive, like a sweet memory, archived and available for the days when nobody is coming.

"Though the fig tree may not blossom; nor fruit be on the vine, though the labor of the olive may fail. And the fields yield no food; though the flock may be cut off from the fold, and there be no herd in the stalls. Yet I will rejoice in the Lord. I will joy in the God of my salvation."

HABAKKUK *3:17–19*

SINGLE SERVING

Are there things you wish you didn't have to do alone? How has God made you feel supported?

The Old New and the New Old

It was a lazy Saturday morning, and I'd taken the liberty of turning off all my phones. I picked strawberries from my garden and tied twine to some unruly tomato branches. I used the strawberries for pancakes.

Earlier, as I sat in my bed looking out the window, I'd seen a rabbit hop past the garden and not even stop after observing the tall marigolds serving as a scarecrow in the center. I could hear the rush of the trees as they yielded to the breeze.

I put on my green garden boots and watered the lawn in my pajamas. Afterward, the smell of dampness, mulch, fertilizer, and soil took me back to the days when I released my mother's hand and ran through a local plant nursery. The crunch of the gravel under my feet was amusing and somehow still familiar even today.

We didn't have much, and much of what we had was old or inexpensive. But we had experiences. I learned to put my hands in the dirt and plant something. I learned that marigolds could grow in the projects. My fascination with the boldness of the color green after a heavy rain began on the steps of our little apartment.

It was a sanctuary.

As I sit in the quiet sanctuary of my home today, I find that same peace. I look out into my backyard, breathe in the summer air, and say to myself, "I am blessed." I exhale with a deep sigh, as though I just settled into a nap.

It's in these moments that the single woman is the envy of the married parent—alone with only her thoughts as a companion; free to run on gravel, plant, create, and, yes, rest; free to make the old new and the new old. What a blessing indeed.

～⌇

"Return to your fortress, you prisoners of hope; even now I announce that I will restore twice as much to you."

ZECHARIAH 9:12

～⌇

SINGLE SERVING

In what ways has being single blessed you? When being single gets old, how do you renew your gratitude?

This Brand of Love

Dozens of handwritten notes are buried either in flowerpots or the ground in my garden. They're prayers, wishes, and dreams that I either symbolically left for dead and buried or hoped the small deposit of my heart would someday blossom into reality. They are love letters written to the Lord about my frustration with singleness, my heartache over bouts of loneliness, and my willingness to surrender to His plan for my life. For this reason, I am a constant gardener.

I rise early to pray and prune. With sweat rolling down my face after a morning run, I cool down with shears in my right hand that click as I tailor a rosebush or cut back an iris. The attention to detail and the love and care paid to each flower, bush, leaf, and bag of soil are my love language. Every labor in the name of this brand of love hardly feels like labor at all. Quite simply, it's who I am at my core. I was made for love, care, and attention. That nurturing spirit, that energy that I leave behind in every corner of my lawn, attracts God's creatures. Baby rabbits nestle in the corners of the house behind my morning-glory trellis, tree frogs hang out by the front door waiting for the insect buffet, and turtles wander into the yard for the same reason. This is my brand of love. This is me loving me.

"And now these three remain: faith, hope and love.
But the greatest of these is love. "

1 CORINTHIANS 13:13

SINGLE SERVING

How are you planting, sowing, and reaping God's love in your life as a single woman?

Laugh on Purpose

Laugh loudly, laugh often, and most important, laugh at yourself.

—Chelsea Handler

God bless our married friends. Where would we be without them? With much sympathy and compassion, they really try to include us whenever possible. A couple whom I'm friends with invited me to join them at a local theater for a modern-dance performance. They had complimentary tickets, and, to avoid a lonely night at home, I gladly accepted their invitation. Little did I know that my seat was four rows away, right next to the other complimentary tickets they gave to another couple they befriended, an adorable pair expecting their second child. The wife was sweet, bubbly, and beautiful, glowing with the fullness of a third-trimester pregnancy. The husband was traditionally handsome with a chiseled jaw, and he was gregarious. Both were kind and polite as I settled into my seat next to the poster children of the life I may never have. Apparently, they were my dates for the night—or maybe I was theirs.

As the dancers warmed up on stage before the big show, the husband observed the enthusiastic performers.

"Well, they're certainly full of energy," he said to his wife.

"Ha! They must not have any children," she quipped, and they both laughed in unison.

You can insert some form of a gut kick here as I sank farther into my seat. Ugh. It was going to be a long night. Still, the performance was lovely, and I imagined a less awkward Friday-night date. Somehow, me in my pajamas wedged between two Yorkshire Terriers didn't seem that bad.

We got to the intermission, and the husband asked, "Do you have any children?"

"No." I smiled, knowing this was not the time to share my child-loss story.

"They're the best! Just you wait and see. But they're work," he offered.

I smiled again, nodding and widening my eyes to affirm his statement.

"It's not that we don't love our toddler," the wife added apologetically. "It's just that we needed a date night. I miss date nights. Honey, don't you remember how we used to date?"

Oh God! I remember when I used to date! Where's a falling stage light or a sudden illness when you need one? At that moment, I would've given anything to escape the land of the happily married with children. Just as I braced myself for the final act, an older woman in the seat behind me tapped me on the shoulder and placed her hand on my jacket that hung over my seat.

She said, "Pardon me, dear. But it's so cold in here. Would you mind if I wear your jacket?"

I couldn't deny an old woman the warmth of my denim jacket. I looked at her, I looked at the poster children of love, and I considered whether I was in hell. No, this was something quite different, some sort of single-woman purgatory. It occurred to me that not only was I the fifth wheel on a double date, I was also playing the part of the man I would like to date. Well, at least chivalry isn't dead—even if I provide it. I genuinely laughed aloud and surrendered my pride along with my jacket.

I can't make this stuff up!

The truth is, every now and again, the universe makes us laugh at the utter ridiculousness of our disappointment with being single. Just like a good friend, I've learned that God has a timely sense of humor, and so should we. It's just as important to celebrate the comedy that comes with the single person's journey as it is to RSVP to our pity party.

~~~

*"A merry heart does good, like medicine.
But a broken spirit dries the bones."*

PROVERBS 17:22

~~~

SINGLE SERVING

Consider a moment when you found the humor in your single journey. What did you learn from that moment?

Picture Imperfect

I believe that happy girls are the prettiest girls. I believe that tomorrow is another day and I believe in miracles.

—AUDREY HEPBURN

We don't always feel how we look. One of my favorite photographs was captured during a valley experience in my dating life. Nursing a broken heart and dreading another round of singleness, I sat in the sand with the waves crashing over me. At that moment, I looked up and laughed, genuinely tickled by the water. The sun was bright as I lifted my eyes underneath my shades and a wide-brimmed hat. A bird flew overhead, soaring effortlessly. I smiled at my laughter. To see something taking flight from that vantage point made me feel free too—absolutely free. It was pure joy, caught on camera. My mother, who'd had the unfortunate burden of bearing witness to my sorrow this particular summer, watched me from a distance and snapped photos with my cellphone as I smiled.

Later, I scrolled through my phone's photo stream and cried tears of joy, astounded by the split-second image of me returning to happiness, returning to myself. The photo of my sun-kissed brown skin garnered plenty of likes on social media, but the caption should've read, "Sad Girl." Little did they know that I had cried every day for a solid month. I was convinced I wouldn't know sunshine and laughter for a long while.

After that day, I would cry some more, but at least I had an image in my mind, a road map to genuine joy and a healed heart. The caption of a single woman's internal image, the photograph of her soul, should say, "I am beautiful. I am happy. More importantly, I am enough."

~⁍

"Weeping may endure for the night,
but joy comes in the morning."

PSALM 30:5

~⁍

SINGLE SERVING

How do you see yourself? How might you capture and appreciate your inner and outer beauty during difficult times?

Get in the Boat

The unknown is hard for a single woman. Frankly, it's hard for any one of us.

With envy and thirst, I scrolled through my social-media news feeds, inundated with images of other people's personal successes: baby photos, marriages, miracle babies, and even remarriages. At times, I tried to broker a deal with God. I cried out to Him, "Tell me if this thing is happening or not!" But faith doesn't work like that. The destination is often a site unseen.

After a relationship that ended with the loss of a child, I drove with my dear friend Martha across the country, from North Carolina to Las Vegas, on the same weekend that would've marked an opulent baby shower. I'd never been a fan of long-distance driving, but somehow, my grief changed with the changing scenery. From the Appalachian Mountains to the tumbleweeds of Texas, we drove to Vegas.

We stood in line at an exclusive nightclub, where we encountered a fortune-teller sitting in a tiny room the size of a closet with crystals dangling from the ceiling and jewel-colored pillows and curtains. Martha's adventurous spirit won over my religious doubt and called me to participate. I'm so glad I did, though. Imagine my surprise when the fortune-teller—in Sin City of all places—began to talk about God. Without knowledge of my story, she gently held my hand, soothed me, and said, "Get in the boat. Get in the boat! There are wings on your back. Get in the boat! The boat is God."

I had no idea that what lay ahead was a gut-wrenching journey through grief, the stripping away of the relationship with my child's father, twenty-four-hour homelessness, major surgery, job loss, job gain, and years of healing. Looking back, it didn't feel good, but it was good for me, as a wise mentor once said.

We don't know what lies ahead. All we have is right now—not even a minute later. So we have to just sail into the mystic, the unknown. Get in the boat. There are wings on your back. Get in the boat. And know that the boat is God.

~⁀

"For we walk by faith, not by sight."

2 CORINTHIANS 5:7

~⁀

SINGLE SERVING

Consider a difficult time during your single journey. Looking back, how might it have been a blessing in disguise?

A Prayer on Waiting

Abba Father,
Thank you for loving me while I seek someone to love.
I don't want to be any man's mother.
I don't want to be his tutor, his teacher, or his mentor.
I don't want to be his doormat.
I don't want to teach, wait, or chase.
I want to be loved as you have designed me to be loved.
Please help me to be the woman you designed me to be.
I want to be a helpmate, his rib, his equal, his friend, his prayer
warrior.
Surely that is worth waiting for, Lord.

*"And the Lord God said, 'It is not good that man should
be alone; I will make him a helper comparable to him.'"*

Genesis 2:18

SINGLE SERVING

Do you find it useful to pray for a husband? Why or why not?
Who are the other "helpers" God has placed in your life?

Love, Patience, and Miracles

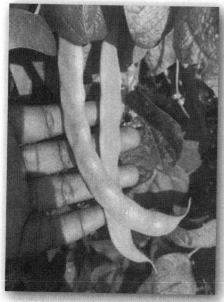

More beans, please! One of my favorite childhood memories is snapping beans with my great-grandmother. She'd sit in her rocking chair with a bucket of fresh-picked beans on one side and a big metal pot for the snapped parts on the other. I'd sit on a small stool facing her, watching her speed and precision. Snap, snap, snap, toss! Every crisp, green pod went from one side to the other in her weathered hands. Nothing went to waste. A simmering pot of beans and the sweet smell of Vidalia onions with a little bacon fat soon followed.

As I pick and snap beans from my garden, I'm reminded of that. I thank God for the harvest, the gathering of all that I've given, poured in, and invested—sometimes with little or no return—for no other reason than to labor in love. This season is not in vain. No, nothing is wasted. Nothing at all.

"Therefore, my beloved brothers and sisters, stand firm. Let nothing move you. Always give yourselves fully to the

work of the Lord, because you know that your labor in
the Lord is not in vain."

1 CORINTHIANS 15:58

SINGLE SERVING

Consider a time when you loved unconditionally without a return on your investment. Looking back, how did your patient endurance pay off?

All That Washes Away

Leave it at the beach.

—Tiffanie Jones Artis

For years, I've sought sanctuary in the comforting waves of the ocean. I would load up my little car and drive two hours to the beach to drown my thoughts—and to hear God. Breakup after breakup, I returned to this place, the place where families, couples, and lone surfers can coexist in peace.

I walked the shore in tears or with an adventurous spirit, armed with a boogie board and childlike enthusiasm. I wrote my son's name in the sand or said a prayer for my heart and let the tide roll in and wash it all away. The surf in the season of singleness can be rough. It involves a great many gains and losses. But we must be equally grateful for all that washes up on shore and all that washes away. Count it all joy.

"The Lord on high is mightier than the thunder of many waters, than the mighty waves of the sea."

Psalm 93:4

SINGLE SERVING

How might you practice peace? What gives you peace in your relationship with yourself and with God?

Spirit of Comparison

The grass is only as green as we keep it.

—NATHAN FEILES

If we allow it, our season of singleness can make us repeated victims of two self-defeating mind-sets: the spirit of comparison and the spirit of lack. In other words, the grass is always greener in someone else's backyard—where we don't live, where we hope to live, where some of us may never live. It manifests in the bittersweet sting of every engagement party, bridal shower, and wedding invitation. It's in the collage of birth announcements, save the dates, and holiday family magnets that litter the sides of our refrigerators.

One night when the spirit of comparison and the spirit of lack gripped me in a chokehold, I jumped from the covers of my bed and ran into my prayer closet (my actual closet). I was armed with a candle, a Bible, and tear-soaked pajamas in the dark of night when God dealt with me.

I had to admit that the unfulfilled desire to be a wife, a mother, and a homemaker had led to years of comparing my life to others, a systemic highlighting of what I'd been diligently praying for yet had not received. I asked God for relief from myself.

At that very moment, I blindly opened my Bible, and the pages fell open to the first chapter of Ecclesiastes. It is often referred to as "The Vanity of Life." Ancient wisdom poured from the page, as this direct message from my Father was deposited in my heart. My grieving soul got quiet and listened to David as he faced the sunset of his life, as he reflected on his journey, as he tried to make sense of it all. Despite his wealth, his personal successes and failures, his loves and losses, he understood there was just one constant that would not disappear in the wind. It would prevail through generations, long after he had become dust. That one constant is the *only* One.

God has told us: everything we need, we already have. Some prayers may or may not be answered. Our abundance will come from Him and Him alone. It will not be fulfilled in the pursuit of things, people, status, or a fabricated public image. It will not be found in someone else's perfectly manicured backyard. It will only be found in the One who has already given us green pastures.

"He makes me to lie down in green pastures."

PSALM 23:2

SINGLE SERVING

In what ways have you compared your life to others? Make a list of all the awesome things about being single. How might you appreciate your life more during a season of waiting?

Acceptance

When conditions are right, acceptance feels like a warm coat. Wear it too early in the season of singleness, and you'll sweat underneath the uncomfortable intensity of a journey that's forced. Intentionally delay its protective covering, and it will seem inadequate against the bitter cold of your choices and circumstance.

No, acceptance is like autumn, a gradual turning of leaves and a gradual letting go. Fall foliage doesn't suddenly burst with amazing color—that would be too overwhelming to our sight. God knows this. So He gently invites the colors of His new canvas to appear. As time slowly passes, there's an ease about the transition and a calm that comes with the completion of this beautiful, painstaking process. Not one step is omitted in this evolution, this path to peace.

One morning, when there's a slight nip in the air, the subtle difference between what *was*, what *is*, and what *could be* will be made clear. That's when you'll reach for your jacket or that favorite weathered sweater and wrap yourself in what's next. Consider it a big hug from yourself.

"He went a little farther and fell on His face, and prayed, saying, 'My Father, if it is possible, let this cup pass from Me; nevertheless, not as I will, but as You will.'"

MATTHEW 6:39

SINGLE SERVING

Are there any aspects of singleness that are hard for you to accept? How might your faith help you to make peace with them?

Do It Yourself

I t was a hard-fought battle between me and a three-way light switch. It had malfunctioned, leaving the foyer light on. I looked at the switch, the switch looked at me, and I thought, "I can do this. I can Google. I can find a DIY video online. I can go to the hardware store and find one of those voltage detector things. I can replace this light switch without electrocuting myself or setting my house on fire. Right?"

The video made the wire removal seem like a piece of cake. But those wires wouldn't budge. I pulled, poked, and prodded to no avail.

The light switch was winning. So was that little voice in my head reminding me that this was a job for a man—specifically a husband. Some women may feel the gut-punching ache of their singleness with every RSVP in wedding invitations, but, for me, it's the absence of a tool-belt hero. From every wet bag of soil I've carried over my shoulder from the driveway to the backyard to that damn light switch, it is physical proof that I am without a helpmate.

My battle with those stubborn wires brought on genuine tears of frustration and memories of exes who had once come to rescue me. I stood in the foyer, feeling defeated, and my ego deflated. Does everything have to be so hard? Lord, when do I get *easy*? It wasn't fair. So I got mad. I jammed a flathead screwdriver into the plastic light switch case and viciously deconstructed it. Piece by piece, the wires gave way. Finally! The theme song to the motion picture *Rocky*, from the scene where the determined fighter makes it to the top of the steps, played in my head. I threw a few air punches at the light switch in a victory dance.

I did it!

I did it.

In that silly moment, I was so proud. In what might be considered a lightbulb moment, it occurred to me that God allowed me to wrestle with myself, my fears, and my frustrations with singleness—not to torture me, but to show me what I'm made of. I had come to my own rescue. I am my best helpmate.

~

"I can do all things through Christ who strengthens me."

PHILIPPIANS *4:13*

~

SINGLE SERVING

In what unexpected ways has being single strengthened you? What valuable skills has singleness allowed you to develop?

Happily Single

Don't misunderstand boredom, for it is truly peace.

—WENDY DANIEL FARMER

Any woman—single or married—should count herself blessed if she has an inner circle of wise women. Two amazing and supportive friends, both named Wendy, come to mind. Out of necessity in conversation (and as a joke), I distinguish them by race. Hence, they lovingly answer to "Black Wendy" and "White Wendy" whenever I call their names.

Years ago, "Black Wendy," an entrepreneurial, tech-savvy preacher's wife, gave me the pearl of wisdom that is the aforementioned quote. "White Wendy," a self-made, hardworking, globe-trotting baller, has served up her brand of wisdom with the high-spirited example of her life. I marvel at her with envy. For her, singleness is her soul, her fabric. She'll tell you she wasn't born with the baby bug, that deep desire to be wrapped in toilet paper or pinned with diapers at a shower. No, for her, the wild winds of adventure call her name. They've carried her to the top of Machu Picchu and Iceland's Godafoss waterfall in the middle of winter. There are exotic beaches that know her name, along with millionaires who are undeniably attracted to her mystique and fierce independence. She charts her own course, and singleness is her ticket. Her *preference* is to travel alone.

As the woman at the diner said in *When Harry Met Sally*, "I'll have what she's having!"

Try as I might, though, I can't wholeheartedly embrace Wendy's brand of unapologetic rejection of the message ingrained in the minds of all little girls from day one: meet a prince, get married, and live happily ever after. My soul will always long for my heart's desire, while Wendy's is constantly evolving as she evolves. I admire that. I admire and love her bold defiance of the sorority of spinsterhood. She's in good company, with the likes of Jane Austen, Oprah, Diane Keaton, and Coco Chanel. Give it time, and I might get there. After all, isn't that what frequent-flyer miles are for?

"Do not be conformed to this world,
but be transformed by the renewal of your mind,
that by testing you may discern what is the will of God,
what is good and acceptable and perfect."

ROMANS 12:2

SINGLE SERVING

Do you think you're called to be single? Make a list of some practical ways being single and traveling alone could be an amazing adventure.

He Need Only Say Be

He need only say, Be, and it is.

—Holy Qur'an

I began to keep track of the names and the number of people I encountered or befriended over the years who had seemingly found love, got engaged, got married, and then started a family. Through Herculean effort or sheer

luck or favor, love had found them. From where I was standing, they made it look effortless. From friends who were divorcées to men who had cheated to a sweet woman who had been proposed to while she was undergoing chemotherapy to the least likely to commit to another person, they all had what I had been praying for. But how? Why them, Lord, and not me? Why have you forsaken me? Why give me the desire only to keep me from it? I've stood within reach of all I witnessed in the joyous photos of other people's lives only to see it slip away. It's human nature to want to know *why*.

Erroneously, I subscribed to the belief that God is handing out gold stars and Facebook-enviable lives for good behavior. But He doesn't love

31

us like that. He loves us unconditionally. Still, I need to look no further than my family tree to know there are walls some people cannot scale and that even good people die alone. My late aunt deeply desired to find true love. Until her last breath, she held fast to her hope for romance. When she was diagnosed with breast cancer at the age of forty-seven, she was a graceful saint who never complained when radiation made her ache to the bone. There was no husband there to hold her hand in the end. She didn't ask the cancer, why me? She only said, "Why *not* me?"

Like my aunt, in the final stage of acceptance, I've started to say to my singleness, "Why *not* me?" When a name or face comes to mind of someone who is married again after a divorce or is having another child after a loss, I remind myself to respect God's sovereignty. It is neither good nor bad. It just is what it is.

Yes, we must do our parts. Our obedience is part of the process. But He need only say, "Be," and it is. If we truly trust Him, His plans, His ways, then the knowledge that our current situation is at least allowed by Him should give us some comfort. He knows—all of it, every detail. It has passed through His hands, and while it may not answer the question why, it certainly defines the *when*. It will happen when He says it will.

~~

"And God said, Let there be light: and there was light."

Genesis 1:3

~~

SINGLE SERVING

Have you ever questioned why you are single?
How might your season of singleness be a part of God's plan for you?

Waiting for Real

Sometimes women on the single journey are treated like patients with a poor prognosis. What's worse are the folks who try to prescribe the cure. I was in the grocery checkout line when an older man stopped to speak to me. I couldn't remember his name, but his face was familiar. He smiled and asked how I was doing, how work was, and if I'd decided to stay in the area. I proudly told him that I was a homeowner, an avid gardener, and the mother of two adorable Yorkies. His expression turned from congenial to bewilderment.

"No *husband*?" he asked, raising an eyebrow. "I guess you're settled in then."

I smiled and gently responded with great restraint, "I guess I am."

As if I had a terminal illness, he quickly offered his condolences and placed his hand on my shoulder, "Oh, don't worry! There's still time."

I wish I had twenty dollars for every time someone asks, "Why aren't you married?" That question, in all its many forms, stings every time. It's not only annoying but also biased. Of course, people mean well. I've learned it's more of a comment than a question. They may actually think you're pretty amazing, and they're genuinely confused about your marital status. Still, it's like asking an infertile couple why they don't have a baby. The question itself puts the onus on the single person, and it suggests that marriage is the ultimate affirmation of a blessed life. A snarky response rooted in statistics, spirituality, or even sexism won't suffice. The question keeps resurfacing though. The single woman is like a museum exhibit under observation. You're either admired or you're the reason behind a few raised eyebrows.

Is she gay? Is she crazy? Is she looking for perfection? No, no, and no. Maybe she's just waiting. Maybe she's holding out hope for God's best. In other words, she's waiting for *real*: Real courage. Real faith. Real love.

~⌒〜

"Trust in the Lord with all your heart, and do not lean on your own understanding. In all your ways acknowledge him, and he will make straight your paths."

PROVERBS 3:5–6

~⌒〜

SINGLE SERVING

If you respond to questions about being single, how might you establish a respectful boundary while demonstrating your faith?

Relationship Ambition

When frustration and loneliness creep in, I gently remind myself of my original life plan. It went something like this: successful career; successful career; and, did I mention, successful career? There was a time when singleness was all I wanted. In fact, I used to have this recurring daydream that kept me motivated while working long hours and holidays early in my career: I stand in a palatial penthouse overlooking a major city skyline (probably New York or Chicago). My attire is tailored, impeccable, and expensive as I hit the play button on my voicemail. I look out at those big-city lights while message after message plays, family and friends desperately trying to reach me but failing. In this dream, I am neither concerned nor feeling guilty. I've reached the apex of my career, and I am satisfied. It is everything.

Ambition requires a clear trajectory. You must not only know where you want to go but precisely how you'll get there. How long you'll stay in one location. What skills you'll attain before moving on to the next. There is no breathing, no pausing. Just huffing and puffing, moving right along, straining toward the next goalpost. For many years, I perfected this skill set, and it served me well professionally. Personally, well, that's another matter. My strategy was lacking. Notice that there were no husband or kids in that daydream. Their absence was hardly worth a mention at the time. That is, until my trajectory started to change. I wanted more. I wanted a family. The mother of a dear friend (who also has an equally demanding and successful career) pointed out the holes in our personal résumés.

"Humph!" she quipped as we lamented about dating while packing up her daughter's kitchen. Like a lot of single women, that successful career had just helped her to buy a new house.

"What about your personal vitae?" my friend's mother asked, pointing out to her thirtysomething daughter and me that our sacrifices had come at a cost. Speaking from a generation when women were considered successful if they'd earned a Mrs. instead of a Ph.D., she sweetly encouraged us to get to work on finding a husband, not a soul mate. She told us to marry whomever; have children; and, if necessary, get divorced.

"At least you'll have a baby. Your personal vitae will show success on paper and in life," she offered. Her daughter, who has a doctorate in the hard sciences, gasped. It was a real clutch-the-pearls moment. It was also brutally honest.

Career ambition is not the same as relationship ambition. We had a plan for our careers, but not much else. Did we lack the same tenacity and ambition in love, or was this just the way it was meant to be? If we tried hard enough, we figured everything would all fall into place—until it didn't. Time passed, relationships failed, hearts broke, and frustration mounted. From online dating to blind dates, the last-minute strategy to get back in the game has yet to pan out.

Looking back, I should've politely embraced the advice from my friend's mother instead of taking it literally to heart. I remember that daydream. I had it all planned out. But we can spend a lot of time convincing ourselves of who we want to be instead of accepting who we are in the season we are in. Be patient with your process. Sometimes God is perfecting love in us. A long season of singleness is never in vain if it is used wisely. It is better to be whole and healed when love finally arrives than to be believe you are when you are not.

~~~

"A man's heart plans his way,
but the Lord directs his steps."

PROVERBS 16:9

~~~

SINGLE SERVING

If you approached finding a husband like building a career, what does your personal resume reveal? Are you ready to be a wife? If so, why? If not, what skills and experience might you need to gain?

Her Own Best Friend

What a lovely surprise to finally discover how unlonely being alone can be.

—Ellen Burstyn

It was a rainy Thursday, and I sat at a tiny, wobbly table at a beach resort located at the very tip of an island. The resort is a popular wedding destination, but on that particular weekend, storms were rolling in, threatening the weekend festivities. I overheard the manager calming the fears of a nervous family at the table next to me. He tells them the legend of the hotel: how in twenty years, it had never rained on a single wedding party. He told them about a bride who insisted on getting married on the beach despite an impending tropical storm. Wide-eyed and hopeful, the family leaned in as he explained how at the moment the ceremony was to start, the skies parted, the sunshine broke through the clouds, and it turned out to be a glorious ritual of love. After the newlyweds said, "I do" and safely made it inside, the pouring rain flooded the beach. Whether fable or fact, he went on to tell them how midway through the reception, a rainbow emerged, giving the wedding party a chance to take their most cherished photographs. It was a sign, he reassured them. It was God's promise of a solid marriage even through the storm. He told them to pray for rain and to wait for the miracle.

Their shoulders relaxed as my fingers quickly jotted down the story on my laptop, ensuring I wouldn't forget the irony of the moment. I was at the resort days ahead of weddings and parties for some much-needed rest and relaxation. My trusted laptop was my only companion. I dined alone. I walked the beach alone. I rented a bike and cycled down unknown streets alone. I rose in the morning with surfers and sea gulls to pray in the direction of the sun—alone. This was also a miracle of sorts. It was a survival skill that some single people struggle to master. It was a demonstration of personal strength and courage. It was the art of self-love when it felt like everyone was watching. *Who is she? Why is she here alone? What's her story?* Oh, how I've imagined countless times what others might have wondered about the single woman at the tiny, wobbly table. May her spirit seem content and at ease. May she exude confidence instead of insecurity. More importantly, may she always know how to be her own best friend.

"Whoever gets sense loves his own soul;
he who keeps understanding will discover good."

PROVERBS 19:8

SINGLE SERVING

In what ways are you a loving, kind, and supportive friend to yourself?

Every. Single. Day.

January 14, 2011. Apparently, it was one of the best days of my life. I know this because I've kept a journal since the fourth grade. I go back to this particular entry not out of nostalgia, but as a reminder: every day, there is magic. Every. Single. Day.

I went hiking that day at a state park. It was beautiful and refreshing—even a bit frightening. A coyote crossed my path, but I didn't panic. I let it pass as I stood still and quietly pivoted, thinking I'd abandon my walk through the woods. But the way I felt, all free, my lungs filled with cold air, I just wanted to keep going. So I did.

By the time I reached the lake, the sun was high, bright, and warm. The lake was still, as it had frozen overnight. I could still hear the rushing water from a nearby dam. It was as quiet as an open space can be. I sat down on a wooden bench, face up toward the sun. My stress and anxiety seemed to melt away. A spirit of gratitude washed over me. Then the show began.

A large blue heron groaned and swooped in, hovering over the water. It glided just above the icy surface with an enviable ease and elegance. I was so appreciative and asked God to show me more. That's when a flock of ducks took flight, and like the cadence of a soft voice, I heard the most delicate flutter of their wings in that big, open quietness. It was all so lovely. I felt emotional, even teary-eyed, because once again, God saw me, and He showed up.

We do not know when the things we desire will arrive. We're human; we get frustrated. But some days the *when* doesn't matter when we *know* God is already there.

~~~

"The Lord, He is the One who goes before you.
He will be with you, He will not leave you nor forsake you;
do not fear nor be dismayed."

DEUTERONOMY *31:8*

~~~

SINGLE SERVING

In what ways does God remind you that He sees you, hears your prayers, and loves you?

#Winning

Don't get stuck on how it really doesn't feel fair.

—MICHELLE MITCHELL

I t's halftime, and the score is Backslider, seven; Faithful, zero.
Let's be honest: sometimes it feels like we're losing. There are times when you wonder if singleness is some form of punishment, an endless purgatory because of something you did. Did we tick someone off on the other side? Like Oprah's holiday giveaway, it's as if God is handing out husbands. We're standing in the audience, cheering, screaming, and jumping like all the other aspiring wives with purity pledges.

"And you get a husband! And you get a husband! And you..."

It's your turn, and a sudden hush sweeps over the crowd. There's an awkward silence.

"You...you get a new car!"

Great! Just what we need—a new car but no one to help pay the taxes. That's what it feels like when it seems that the blessing bucket never makes it to our aisle. We look around in the pews on Sunday morning and find countless examples of married couples who haven't always made the wisest or most righteous of choices. A dear friend who has faithfully served the Lord since childhood is no closer to marriage than another friend whose adventurous dating history ultimately led her to the love of her life. How can that be? It just doesn't seem fair. That's if you believe in merit-based love given out by a merit-based God.

Thankfully, He doesn't love us that way. Otherwise, we'd get far more than a perceived purgatory for our thoughts and actions. Our choices can alter our path, but I believe nothing can alter God's plan. The way we get to the destination can be changed or delayed, but not the destination itself. God's will is God's will. His sovereignty is His sovereignty. We often ask, why her and not me? Why them and not us? The better question is, is marriage God's will for me? *Ouch.*

That's a tough one. It means that no matter how righteous we think our résumé is compared to someone who has received the blessing we think we deserve, God is neither handing out nor withholding helpmates based solely on our deeds. This is not to suggest reckless abandonment of the law for single people (1 Corinthians 7). Faithfulness is ultimately rewarded. But *how* is up to God. When it feels like we're the captain of a losing team, remember that His grace *is* enough. Stay in the game. After all, it's only halftime.

"Let us not become weary in doing good, for at the proper time we will reap a harvest if we do not give up."

GALATIANS 6:9

SINGLE SERVING

When you see others receiving the blessing of marriage and family, do you experience feelings of jealousy? How might your faith help you to be more supportive and less judgmental? How can your faith keep you encouraged?

Hope a Day

From spread eagles to splits to round-offs, every year that I tried out for cheerleading, I made the squad. Every year, including my final season as a high school senior, I launched into a fit of teenage angst and fears immediately after tryouts. I cried, fearful that *this* time I wouldn't succeed. Back then, my hometown announced the names of the lucky cheerleaders on the radio. I couldn't even listen. I waited for someone else to tell me. I talked myself out of my own success before I allowed myself to consider that it could all work out—again. I wish I could tell you I no longer think this way. Call me a pessimistic optimist with a dash of realist.

"You've been this way your whole life," my mother offered, year after year.

If the struggle was real when it came to cheerleading, imagine what I was like when it came to dating. Did he like me? I mean, *really* like me, or was he just being nice? Is this going somewhere? Could he be The One? Probably not. Maybe? How exhausting! Deeply insecure, I was trying to spare myself the crushing disappointment if things didn't work out. If I failed to make the cheerleading squad, at least I could claim I knew it all along. If the relationship didn't meet its full potential, at least I had predicted it. Oh dear! Someone needed to place her belief and expectations on God and far less upon herself. Instead, I was buying tickets for a train that had not yet arrived.

I know now that there's nothing to lose in hoping. The alternative is no better. Studies suggest faith and hope can improve the prognosis in seriously ill patients. Why couldn't it work for matters of the heart? Hope, in the very least, increases endorphins, according to researchers. If we're going to run the race, let's at least remain motivated. A dose of hope a day will keep that pesky pessimist away!

~

"And now, O Lord, for what do I wait?
My hope is in you."

PSALM 39:7

~

SINGLE SERVING

Are you insecure about being single? How might your prayer life help you develop more trust in God?

The Husband Upstairs

O Romeo, Romeo! Wherefore art thou Romeo?

—WILLIAM SHAKESPEARE

In the absence of my own children, I get the chance to play honorary aunt to a host of lovable, adorable, smart, and downright hilarious kids who belong to my dearest friends. Early on a Sunday morning, a family emergency left  the inquisitive Isabella in my care as her parents tended to other matters. I strapped her petite four-year-old frame in her car seat, and we headed to church, singing the likes of Taylor Swift and the soundtracks of animated movies. I hurried her along to the children's ministry. She pouted and played on my emotions with crocodile tears, but I was a veteran aunt. I soothed her, kissed her forehead, and waved good-bye on my way to the adult sanctuary.

Afterward, I scooped her up like a child much younger than her age, resting her on my hip as we walked back to the car. On the way to breakfast, we swapped stories about the lessons of the day. She told me how she learned that God loves her no matter what. I smiled, pleased that her parents are depositing pearls of faith in her heart that will help her when she's my age. Somewhere between the quick trip to Target for a toy and the drive-through of McDonald's, out of the blue, unmotivated, and quite possibly divinely scripted, a question came out of the mouth of this babe.

"Auntie Tam, where's your husband?"

My head turned to the back seat to look at the sweet face from which this sincere curiosity came. She'd never met any of my boyfriends, but she'd certainly witnessed her parents school me in the ways of marriage many times before.

"Well, Bells." I choose my words wisely, holding back laughter. "That's a good question. I don't know where he's at. If you find him, will you let me know?"

Geesh! I was thinking that even a toddler knew something was missing from this picture frame. I laughed to myself, knowing this was one of those moments when the universe was laughing at me.

"Auntie Tam, what about upstairs in your house?" she offered innocently. "Did you check upstairs? Maybe he's up there?"

I glanced in the rearview mirror at her intense facial expression. I'd long believed that Isabella was an old soul in a child's body. As a one-year-old, she demanded ice water with a spoon during her meals, like an old woman. I told her that she wasn't fooling me and that I knew her secret: she was a forty-year-old woman at birth.

"You know, Bells, that's a good idea." I smiled back at her. "When we get home, we'll look upstairs for my husband."

"I bet he's up there," she added, convinced that she'd solved the mystery.

Perhaps she had—if, by "upstairs," she really meant he'll come from heaven.

~

"May the God of your father help you; may the Almighty bless you with the blessings of the heavens above..."

GENESIS 49:25

~

SINGLE SERVING

Are you open to finding love in unexpected places? What steps might you take to keep your heart open?

An Open Heart

There are some things that happen in life that you never recover from.

—Essie Lee Underwood

It was my grandmother's birthday, and she was in good spirits as we chatted over the phone. She's a talker, and I have the dead phone batteries to prove it. Marathon conversations are her expertise, which is why she's an amazing storyteller. Like Charles Dickens, her narrative can spin off into various secondary plots only to be seamlessly tied together in the end. Similarly, her life is a series of adventures and misadventures.

"Tamara, when you're down, you're down. When you're up, you're up," she told me. "But when you're up against a Gibbs, you're upside down!"

Spoken like a true survivor who had endured much in her eighty years. Through the loss of childhood innocence and the loss of two adult children, music and dancing had been her escape as a young woman. Back in the day, it wasn't uncommon to find her and her girlfriends in St. Louis or Memphis, screaming at the live performances of legendary artists. She even has an authentic photo of Elvis leaning against a car, smiling in her direction. There's a story behind it that she won't tell. Indeed, she has lived…and loved.

Eleven babies are proof of her multiple attempts at a happy union. She never married though. It wasn't from a lack of trying. Now she reminisced with me on the phone on this particular night about my grandfather's wavy hair and the way he polished their children's shoes. More than a half century of singleness, and she *still* loves love. Sigh.

Make sure you know you tried. Keep an open heart even during miles of heartache. Always.

~⁓

*"Rejoice in hope, be patient in tribulation,
be constant in prayer."*

ROMANS *12:12*

~⁓

SINGLE SERVING

Do you believe love never fails? How can disappointment strengthen your faith?

Special Delivery

Love's in need of love today. Don't delay. Send yours in right away.

—Stevie Wonder

There's a lone mailbox just after the bend on a secluded beach. Legend has it that the person who maintains it prays for the letters to God that are left there. I pulled back the metal door, and there were weathered composition books and a single ink pen inside. The pages were full of hopes, dreams, desires, victories, and failures. I willingly added my name to the pile. My letter was one page and signed, "With Love, God's Daughter First."

In my letter, I thanked God for the sometimes-difficult season of singleness. I told Him that I've learned to count it all as joy. I thanked him for being my provider and my redeemer. I thanked him for whoever takes the time to read these prayers put to paper. As I placed the composition book back in its rightful place, I rested my hand on the top of the mailbox. I stopped thinking about me, and, instead, I thought of others—all of those souls who happened upon the mailbox, eager for a miracle, like me. I prayed aloud without a care for who was listening and waiting for a turn to make a submission. I prayed for every name and every petition in the mailbox. I prayed that they would get the answer they needed. I prayed that the person who was doing God's work in this way wouldn't grow weary of his or her assignment. I prayed I wouldn't ever become so focused on my selfish desires that I lost sight of the plight of others. I prayed I would always take the time to not only fervently seek unconditional love, but to also send it out.

~⁀

"And the Lord restored the fortunes of Job, when he had prayed for his friends. And the Lord gave Job twice as much as he had before."

JOB 42:10

~⁀

SINGLE SERVING

Focusing on more than your heart's desire, consider creating a prayer list. Whom or what else might you pray for? How might you improve your prayer life?

Sleeping Promises

There is an ethereal beauty in the winter landscape, along with the sleeping promises of what is to come.

—Phyllis Hoffman DiPiano

The North Carolina beach in the dead of winter is the oddest thing. Sea gulls still fly, tourists still walk the shoreline, and surfers still obey the call of the ocean, but it doesn't have that same energy or rhythm that summer seems to bring. It's as if everything is frozen, perfectly preserved, just waiting for the return of the warm summer sun. Doesn't the season of singleness sometimes feel the same way? When there are no prospects, when no one is calling or texting, it's as if the heart is encased in amber. It's still visible, and still beating and beautiful, yet it's suspended in a moment of time that we fear could go on forever. It's the in-between time that's the hardest—the deafening quiet, the undisturbed routine of day-to-day activities. Eventually, we settle in and enjoy the scenery. The beach may be chilly, but it's exclusive. It's as if it's all mine, and it is enough. It's right at that moment when we begin to see the blessing in our circumstances, when we truly appreciate what's happening underneath the surface, that spring finally arrives. The phone rings or dings with a text, a coffee date turns into lunch,

lunch into dinner, and the warmth of the sun returns with the promise
of what is to come.

~‿୬

*"But they who wait for the Lord shall renew their
strength; they shall mount up with wings like eagles; they
shall run and not be weary; they shall walk and not faint."*

ISAIAH 40:31

~‿୬

SINGLE SERVING

What do you think God has in store for you? Are you willing to
wait for it?

Pick Up Your Horn

Heartache to heartache, we stand. No promises, no demands.

—Pat Benetar

If Pat Benatar thinks love is a battlefield, then singleness can be a minefield. Like a good soldier waiting to be deployed into someone else's heart, you're joyfully walking along, making progress, celebrating yourself, delighting in the Lord, and then the next minute—*Boom*! For any number of reasons, hopes can be dashed, and dreams can be dismantled. Confusion and chaos may even creep in. Whether it's something as minor as a disappointing date, the loss of a relationship, or an unexpected life change, it can leave the battle-weary single woman asking, "What am I fighting for?"

The short answer is a helpmate, a husband, a soul mate. The deeper, more immediate answer is something entirely different. God is giving you the opportunity to conquer yourself.

After one of my greatest losses and disappointments, there was a long season of patient endurance. Each day, my only goal was to get up. That's it. That alone was an achievement. Just to open my eyes, roll out of bed, get dressed, take the day by the hand, and walk it out. This required releasing myself from either the intended or unintended outcome of my day. In an act of true surrender, I retired my camouflage-wearing representative and, instead, walked in a spirit of transparency, wounds and all. If someone asked how my day was, I abandoned the customary "I'm good" or "I'm well" in exchange for a brief yet honest response like "I'm hanging in there" or "I'm all right."

My task was no longer to please other people, to meet their expectations of me, or even to please my perfectionist-prone self, but rather to please God. It was my way of boasting my infirmities as the apostle Paul said. I was shouting like Abraham, "Behold, here I am!" I may have lost a battle or two along the way of this adventurous and challenging journey, but the war was still raging.

Staying in the fight is half the battle. There are times when unanswered prayers and unfulfilled dreams become too heavy to carry, hopes too hefty to bear. You can erroneously think laying it all down, temporarily setting it aside, is a sign of defeat. Not so! It's an acknowledgement that your human limitations will no longer allow you to carry it—for a season or two or three, or for whatever length of time is required. But know this: every tear, every prayer, and every desire is on record in heaven. Just when you think all is lost, hope will fall fresh on you again! Until then, pick up your horn and fill it with oil (1 Samuel 16), or pick up your staff (Exodus 4:4). Like an obedient soldier, get up and be accounted for. Answer the roll call. Honor the pulse and the purpose each and every day with your willingness to be fully present.

~

"Let us not become weary in doing good, for at the proper time we will reap a harvest if we do not give up."

GALATIANS 6:9

~

SINGLE SERVING

What difficult storms have you weathered? How did your faith help you to stay motivated? What Scripture kept you going?

Ticktock!

Tell you what you should do when you get up in the morning. Look yourself in the mirror and say, "I love me!"

—Mary Mary

Another one bites the dust. After a few dates and an embarrassing incident at a dinner party, it was obvious we were not a good fit. While I thought I was leaving the situation with honesty and compassion, it didn't soften the blow or prevent him from taking offense. In a quick-tempered way, my date shot back at me. His exact words escape me, but he implied that time was running out for an old bird like me. He warned me that I would be wise to recognize that he was a good man. I recall snapping back with the declaration that, with or without a husband, I would still die with a contented heart. I know; I know. That was the best I could do in a pinch. Since the fifth grade, my comebacks never packed any heat. I'd be less than honest if I didn't admit his words stung. It's the thing most single women at a certain age begin to fear, or rather *hear*. Ticktock! Ticktock! Time's running out! Ticktock!

That was ten years ago. At this writing, I am forty-two and proud of it.

My first strands of silver emerged while I was in graduate school in my midtwenties. I earned every strand. Even when doctors told me my biological clock had prematurely run out in my thirties, I was never a woman fighting against her years. As if strolling on the beach, I still take the seasoned woman by the hand and walk with her and converse with her. She has much to teach me about the sands of time.

57

Rewind the clock back to the age of thirty-two. I'd remind myself that I didn't have to try so hard. I would encourage myself to be more mindful of where I spent my time and with whom. With my hands firmly planted on the shoulders of my younger self, and our eyes locked, I would strongly advise her to take great care of her heart. Otherwise, she would have to learn the hard way that everything originates from it.

Dial it back ten more years, and I would rein in my younger self's romantic ideology and budding addiction to perfection. She would need to know that she and her potential soul mate required friendship over fireworks, faith over flesh. I would also tell her to save every penny, pack light, and travel the world. The broader her horizons, the farther her eye could see, the wider the net she would cast in the search for love.

I would sit with the twelve-year-old me in the tree that she'd often pretend was a prince. I would affirm the fairy tale, the original vision. "He's out there waiting," I'd tell her. Let him find you. But just in case you get lost, there's still time to choose.

"Blessed is the one who finds wisdom, and the one who gets understanding, for the gain from her is better than gain from silver and her profit better than gold. She is more precious than jewels, and nothing you desire can compare with her. Long life is in her right hand; in her left hand are riches and honor. Her ways are ways of pleasantness, and all her paths are peace."

PROVERBS 3:13–18

SINGLE SERVING

If you could go back in time, what advice might you give yourself at different stages of your life? What Bible verse or quote might you offer yourself at various ages?

Dramatic Rescue

Don't you like a last-minute rescue? It certainly makes for a great suspense scene in a movie! If I were the heroine in this biopic, nothing would make me happier than if God swooped down in the eleventh hour, the last inning of the series, or the last round of the finals, and hand delivered my heart's desire. *Bam*! A husband, a soul mate, and a loving witness to my life. This is totally within the Lord's power. He is the author of time. He did it for Hezekiah.

Picture the young king lying on the bed, on the verge of death. Tears of disappointment flow as he turns his face to his bedroom wall and cries out to God. He reminds the Lord that he's been a faithful servant. His request for relief is made with a sincere heart. Our merciful God hears the defeat in his voice and decides there will be an alternate ending. With all the power of heaven, the Lord turns back time just for Hezekiah. In the eleventh hour, in the last inning, in the final round, Hezekiah is rescued. God's infinite grace and mercy arrive at the exact moment he needs it most.

Years may pass, but the will of God trumps all. There's always time. There's always time. There's always time. Never forget that.

"Then Isaiah said, 'This is the sign to you from the Lord, that the Lord will do the thing which He has spoken...'"

ISAIAH *20:9*

SINGLE SERVING

Do you feel as though you've wasted or lost valuable time? How might you use your faith to reframe your perspective? Like Hezekiah, write down a prayer request and say it out loud.

Land of What Could Be

I love that final scene in *Sixteen Candles* when Molly Ringwald's character, Samantha, has just emerged from inside the church to retrieve her sister's wedding veil, only to discover that she's missed the newlyweds' send-off. Her heart sinks, and her head drops in disappointment. Her family has already forgotten about her—again. It's at that moment on the church steps that she resigns herself to being a castaway. But there, in the distance, with cars slowly driving away, a teenager's answered prayer is serendipitously revealed. It's Jake, leaning against his red Porsche. He's been waiting for her the entire time.

We don't know if our Jake is coming, but we do know there's always a chance he is. If he hasn't yet, never stop believing in even the tiniest possibility. Never stop believing in fairy-tale beginnings and magic. There's nothing wrong with escaping to the Land of What Could Be. Love is so worth it. It feels like sunshine after a long winter. It is both oxygen and helium, feeding every cell, taking you to higher heights. It's an endless source of laughter. It is courage and strength. It is everything when it's with the right person and God's will. That is still worth dreaming about and praying for.

There have been seasons when I've had to restore my hope in love one romance movie at a time. My Sunday night ritual consists of a bubble bath and a movie. For months, I watched a romantic film while soaking in the tub. From Larenz and Nia in *Love Jones* to Noah and Ally in *The Notebook* to Ronald and Cindy's lawn-mower ride into the sunset in *Can't Buy Me Love*, I laughed, sighed, cheered, and cried for the heroine, because I could see myself in her. I suspended any hint of disbelief—if only for two hours.

Commit to memory every sappy line from a movie, every love lyric from a song, every stanza of poetry. Wish on stars; sing to the moon if you must. Go ahead. I dare you.

~⁊

"And let us not grow weary while doing good, for in due season we shall reap if we do not lose heart."

GALATIANS 6:9

~⁊

SINGLE SERVING

What fun ritual might you create for times when you feel your faith is fading while waiting?

That Still, Small Voice

There's always a storm brewing. Always. That's life. There are downpours of difficulty along with the warmth of beautiful sunshine. So it's best to carry a sturdy umbrella. None of us gets out of this life without feeling the impact of raging winds that flip up our parasol, leaving us scrambling for cover and drenched in the rain. None of us.

During a difficult season of singleness, the winds that blew in through my circumstances forced me to reevaluate my entire life. I had to make firm decisions about what was going to truly make me happy. I was earning great money in a rewarding, yet demanding, career that had consumed most of my existence. Still, it was of little consolation when my heart yearned to be a free spirit, a writer, a teacher, a wife, and a mother. Like a howling wind, the greater my sadness over the unfulfilled dreams, the harder it became to hold on to what I did have. I felt myself losing my grip on both gratitude and grit.

At the time, I was weathering increased stress on the job, worrying about my financial future should I make a much-needed career change, and wrapping my head around the possibility of a frightening health diagnosis. Looking back, I couldn't fully appreciate the blessing of the moment because I was overwhelmed by situational depression, anxiety, fear, confusion, and desperation. A storm was brewing inside and outside—literally and figuratively. It had rained nonstop for eleven days. The local weather forecast warned of flash flooding, high winds, and downed trees in the saturated ground, which could lead to power outages. This was the week I contemplated my resignation, walked through the doors of a cancer center to see a blood specialist, and discovered that the roof of my new home had sprung a leak. I put a pot under the drip. I was drowning.

But there was a break in the rain one Sunday morning. I opened the back door to let out my dogs. I'm notorious for slipping into my green boots and stepping into my garden (in my pajamas) to pick something, only to get carried away doing actual garden work. I only intended to pull two green peppers, and then I started to remove weeds and debris from around the collard-green sprouts that were breaking through the soil. I'd been meaning to pull up some withered pole beans, but life had become a distraction. My hand wrapped around the base of the vine, and I pulled it up at the root.

That's when I heard it: that still, small voice.

"Are you just going to *die* on the vine?"

The question was gentle, yet piercing in my ears, and it was followed by another challenge.

"Don't you know I *am* the vine?"

There, in my green boots and pajamas in the garden, I'd received a reminder from God. Whether in the garden, in the storm, in the wind and the rain, or in the beautiful sunshine, He is with me—always. Always.

In that moment, I vowed to be a face turned up in the rain. I had to make the choice to not wither and die on the vine. I made the choice, because I knew He would not let me wither away. It turned out that I had low iron and not blood cancer. I went on an interview for a new job. The leak stopped when the rain stopped. It was fixed, and I was no longer drowning.

"I am the true vine, and My Father is the vinedresser. Every branch in Me that does not bear fruit He takes away; and every branch that bears fruit He prunes, that it may bear more fruit. You are already clean because of the word which I have spoken to you. Abide in Me,

and I in you. As the branch cannot bear fruit of itself,
unless it abides in the vine, neither can you,
unless you abide in Me."

JOHN 15

SINGLE SERVING

Consider carving out time during your day for a few minutes of quiet reflection. Give it a try and make note of what you "hear" during silent meditation.

Bridal Bouquet

There's a photo that always reminds me that life is still full of little, pleasant surprises—especially when you least expect them. There's a hilarious image of me with my arms stretched out, my hands open, my mouth in awe, and my eyes as wide as two fried eggs. Inside the frame, I am forever suspended in midcatch of a wedding bouquet. My facial expression is that of a priceless moment of sheer surprise. My purple bridesmaid's dress matches the floral glory headed my way. Ironically, I was forced to participate in this reception ritual. I had to be dragged out onto the dance floor. As if it wasn't bad enough being a bridesmaid at forty, I was even more embarrassed to stand in a circle of younger women, beaming with the hope of marriage. I strategically stood in the back of the ravenous pack of bachelorettes. I intentionally let my focus drift elsewhere as we waited for the bride's toss that I was certain someone would catch well before it ever reached me.

Like a slow-motion scene in a movie, that thing soared right over the heads of several Air-Jordan-leaping women and into my unsuspecting, unwilling arms. Damn! Now I'd have to wait and see if this timeless tradition would work in my favor, I thought. *What if it didn't?* I wondered. Then what? What of the disappointment? Still, I couldn't deny that there was something serendipitous about that moment. It was as if fate picked me out of a crowd of desperate damsels and said, "I choose you."

That's a good feeling—to be chosen. It's like the first time a boy asks you to dance or a grown man asks to date you exclusively. I remember that photo when my heart needs a little pick-me-up, a little reminder that anything is possible—especially when I least expect it.

~

"Are not five sparrows sold for two pennies? Yet not one of them is forgotten by God. Indeed the very hairs of your head are all numbered. Don't be afraid; you are worth more than many sparrows."

LUKE *12:6–7*

~

SINGLE SERVING

What serves as a reminder to you that anything is possible, especially when you least expect it?

Genetically Single

Get all you can, and can all you can get.

—Mary Lee Wooley

There's a genealogy behind my singleness. It's almost a family-tree tradition. My grandmother had many great loves (and eleven children), yet she never married. My mother, a beautiful, intellectual siren, also never married. A host of aunts and uncles, all of them great catches, are unmarried. I used to think it was a curse, some kind of hex from long before I came into existence. I have imagined heroically breaking the invocation spoken over one of my ancestors who must have crossed a medicine woman long before the Diaspora or in some cotton field in Alabama. The cycle would end with me, I had vowed. But it didn't. It wasn't for a lack of trying though.

The truth is there's no curse or hex. It's just life—a combination of family patterns, societal statistics, and lottery-like luck. Despite the odds, my continued efforts comfort me rather than disappoint me. I'm not operating in the spirit of desperation, but instead determination to find a spiritual and emotional equal. At least I can always look back and say that I tried. A dear friend once told me that love may find me later rather than sooner in life. When I see newlyweds in their forties, fifties, and sixties, I'm inspired. It makes me wholeheartedly believe in love as God intended it—even in the absence of it. Love never fails. Love will find a way. Love conquers all. Whatever the cliché, may it grow like sweet fruit on your family tree.

"Be patient, therefore, brothers, until the coming of the Lord. See how the farmer waits for the precious fruit of the ear, being patient about it, until it receives the early and the late rains. You also, be patient."

JAMES 5:7–8

SINGLE SERVING

What relationship patterns have you noticed in your family? Are there successful marriages, divorces, or singleness? What choices have you made to create or continue your family's relationship tradition?

Don't Try; Just Trust

A ball or two gets by everyone. Sometimes they're supposed to.

—L. WILLIAMS

Don't try. Just trust.

I know; it's easier said than done. On my morning power prayer walk, I carry three-pound weights in my hands, forcing my aging knees to keep pace with the runner I used to be. I'm earnest and focused, gripping the weights as if they're my life. I can feel the tension in my fingers wrapped around the small dumbbells. I can do this: push myself to the limit, so that I might be healthy and let go of frustration before the workday begins. I need to maintain my weight. I need to feel good about myself. My reward is an antistress endorphin rush at the end of my self-imposed race.

Push, push, try, and try! With that same intensity, I often attack being unmarried, without kids, and over forty. I don't want to be a cliché: Two dogs, no man. Demanding career, no man. A lot of love to give, but no man. "There must be something wrong with her," I assume people are whispering. Gripping my life, my self-esteem, and my public image, I would take matters into my own hands. I would become Super Single! She's all good. See? She's smiling, unaffected by loneliness, the trail of failed relationships, and cooking for many yet dining for one.

But all that trying to remain positive and optimistic requires effort and energy. Crying and lamenting also requires energy. Hurt and anger require energy. Keeping the faith demands energy. Keeping a record of a mistake or two or three also demands effort and energy. Taking care of yourself, your kids, your job, your spiritual life, your home, your finances—it all needs tending to at one stage or another, or all at the same time. It requires work, but to what end if all that racing leaves you exhausted—or worse, depleted? Just let it be. Keeping everything in your grip can lead to one very sore hand.

Don't try so hard. Just trust. Breathe, if only for a few minutes. Download Billy Joel's "Vienna" and be still.

But if you still insist upon trying, try sitting with God.

*"And the Lord, He is the One who goes before you.
He will be with you, He will not leave you nor forsake you;
do not fear nor be dismayed."*

DEUTERONOMY 31:8

SINGLE SERVING

What areas of your life are a challenge to surrender to God? In what ways might you trust more in God's plan for your life?

Nothing but the Water

It was the day after my forty-second birthday, and I was eager to hear a word at a church I'd been visiting. We got there, and the sermon was about baptism. *Been there, done that,* I thought. But this wasn't one of those fiery condemnation messages that convince the new believer to be immediately dumped in the holiest of water to be right with God. Instead, this message was also about the seasoned saint. It was an encouraging call for even the mature believer to become new and improved, whole and healed.

With my original baptism certificate neatly tucked inside my Bible ever since I was twenty-one years old, I already knew I had proof of my salvation. There was no need for a repeat performance, I thought. Yet I could not shake this feeling that He was calling me back to the water. I could not deny the urge to get up from my seat and obey this seemingly irrational prompting in my spirit. I could hear that still, small voice say, I *am* His bride.

I handed my mother my purse and headed to the sanctuary doors, where friendly volunteers had already received dozens of baptismal candidates. I asked the first friendly face, "Am I too late?" She smiled and ushered me to the next station where T-shirts and shorts were waiting. I picked a stall in the bathroom to change into my new garments. I quickly ripped off my clothes as if I were ripping my spiritual flesh; I was happy to suit up for my date with God, grateful for the chance to renew my vows.

"I'm coming," I declared in a moment of complete obedience.

Nothing else mattered at that moment: Not finding the love of my life. Not marriage. Not having a family. Not my career. Not money. It was nothing but the water. I was His, and He was mine. I let my body go limp in an act of surrender as the pastor took me under. I emerged from the depths of the outdoor pool with the sun in my eyes.

There, in front of a crowd of complete strangers, I rededicated myself to my faith walk, to my partnership with God. Yes, it was spontaneous. But it was my continued commitment to courageously see this journey through to the end—with or without the desires of my heart.

~~9

*"His mother said to the servants,
'Do whatever he tells you.'"*

JOHN 2:5

~~9

SINGLE SERVING

How can you demonstrate your obedience to God in your season of waiting?

Picture Frame

Without the right frame, you can't see the picture.

—J. Jennings

Holidays are hard. Not always, but they can be. Especially if you allow them to serve as reminders that you're suspended somewhere between where you were and where you want to be. I've dreamed of a large granite breakfast bar in the middle of my kitchen where my kids will sit,  eager to eat my food. I serve up a delicious Christmas breakfast, much to my husband's delight. We'll open our presents in our pajamas and take silly selfies to mark the occasion. All of this activity is just a preview of the magnificent celebration ahead. Later in the day, we'll host a dozen or so family members and friends who are eager to eat another delicious meal that I've prepared. There will be laughter and loosened belt buckles by the time dessert hits the table. It's family. It's home. It's hearth. It's the polar opposite of being single.

If I'm lucky enough to have the holiday off from work, I can get out of bed when I want. I can linger in my pajamas with a "yuck mouth" all day long, with only two Yorkies to offend (and their breath smells just as bad as mine). If I want to dine with a big brood of people, I have a host of friends whose families I can rent for the day. There have been a dozen Easter Sundays, Thanksgivings, and Christmases where they've saved a seat at their tables for me. Like an adopted family member, they give me a warm plate, a gift, and a hug on my way out the door. It fills me with both humility and gratitude. And yes, sadness—at times.

This is when we must reframe. Both the dream and the reality, in this instance, are the same. If the goal is to play hostess to a family, we can still do that! Whether it's volunteering at a soup kitchen or serving at your dining room table. One Thanksgiving, my mother helped me prepare a meal for ten people. I decided to feed one of my best friends and her family, who have graciously invited me to dine with them every holiday. We prepared turkey and duck along with about six side dishes. The tablecloth was a country plaid. The dinnerware was classic white, simple but classy in contrast with the southern Mason jar mugs for our beverages.

I was so proud as we stood around the table, holding hands to pray for my home, our food, and my labor of love that were provided by God. Tears came to my eyes at the beautiful, bountiful blessing that is family. No matter who or what is in the picture, frame it with gratitude and love.

~⁹

"Give thanks in all circumstances; for this is the will of God in Christ Jesus for you."

1 THESSALONIANS 5:18

~⁹

SINGLE SERVING

Consider the things about being single that trouble you. How might you reframe your perspective to see (and receive) the blessing?

76

God's Promise

(According to Psalm 23)*

1. He will guide you, if you follow.
2. Your needs will be met.
3. He will make provisions for you.
4. He offers peace.
5. He won't lead you astray.
6. He will restore your soul.
7. You need not fear evil.
8. He will protect you and keep you from harm.
9. He will promote you despite your enemies.
10. He will give you an anointing.
11. You will be blessed beyond what you imagined.
12. Goodness and mercy will follow you.
13. You will dwell in heaven for ever and ever.

SINGLE SERVING

Consider each promise in Psalm 23. For each promise, write down an experience where God delivered on His promise to you.

---

* Faith, hope, and love included. Self-limiting beliefs not allowed.

You're Not His Rib

There's another kind of love, one that gives you the courage to be better than you are—not less than you are. One that makes you feel anything is possible. I want you to know that you can have that. I want you to hold out for it. I want you to know that you deserve it.

—*NIGHTS IN RODANTHE* (MOTION PICTURE)

"You have to know when you're *not* his rib." These are words of wisdom from a friend and mentor. We can't wholeheartedly talk about making peace with singleness without making peace with disappointment and heartache over failed attempts at love. Lord knows, I've broken my spirit and hopes on many promising men who needed me to be less so that they could feel blessed. It took years to learn that is not the kind of love worthy of the mutual sacrifice that comes with a real relationship, a real marriage. It's also not a consolation prize when you grow weary of your own company. Sometimes the concessions we make for companionship seem reasonable in the moment until the reflection in the mirror is no longer recognizable.

Holding out is hard, but it's worth the value of your heart and your soul. They are priceless. Every fiber of your being deserves God's best. This is why contentment in singleness is critical. Without it, a woman is incapable of discerning the subtle difference between a good man and a good husband. There is a difference. There are plenty of good, honorable, hardworking men. Their résumés are impressive; their accomplishments make them irresistible. Their faith in the Lord is palpable. But will they hold your hand in a storm? Is he a man with footsteps you would willingly follow in sinking sand? Pretty on paper makes for an ugly union. Be wise, girlfriend. Be wise, and know that being smart, beautiful, faithful, and hardworking makes you a rare rib. A rib forced to fit will bend until it breaks.

"The man said, 'This is now bone of my bones and flesh of my flesh; she shall be called woman for she was taken out of man.'"

GENESIS *2:23*

SINGLE SERVING

Consider your past and current relationship(s). What's been your pattern? Is there anything you might do differently?

Married Sister Friends

Did you ever know that you're my hero?

—BETTE MIDLER

tucked my cell phone between my shoulder and my ear as I juggled bags of makeup, electronic equipment, and my laptop as I walked from the garage into the house.

"Uh-huh. Uh-huh. Yes, girl! That's right," I declare into the phone during a delicate balancing act between my house key and my belongings. "Absolutely!"

Meanwhile, she was literally holding her phone outside the car window with her fingers positioned so that she wouldn't lose the signal driving into her neighborhood. From cheerleading to complaining, it became our after-work ritual. These counseling sessions were an affirmation of two kindred spirits, working and grinding in a demanding career. They were also a testament of our faith, not only in the God we serve in every assignment, but also in one another.

"I just want you to know that I am standing on your shoulders," she quietly said to me. "You are my sister. And I love you."

There's no crying in our profession. A stiff upper lip is a must, especially for a woman. But in these encouraging conversations night after night, we could be our most authentic selves. Strong, yet vulnerable. Smart, yet overwhelmed. Determined, yet tired.

This sacred circle of mutual love and respect leaves no room for such female foolishness as insecurity, envy, jealousy, and cattiness. That's not what you submit to in the presence of real womanhood, grace, and grit. It's a celebration, not a competition. Within that circle is a mirror, a face that looks right back at yours, that knows your walk and willingly walks alongside you. Your lives may not be mirror images, but in friendships like these, you just *know*.

When she looks at me, she sees faith, professional accomplishment, and fortitude in the face of adversity. But when I look at her, I see the life I had always dreamed of: marriage, family, successful career. I cannot help but smile.

"You are everything that I ever wanted to be," I tell her, and then I playfully crown her with a new nickname. "Look at you, T. P.! Total package!"

From marathon runner to mother to wife to formidable journalist in the field, she is not walking, but rather *sprinting* in her purpose. It is like watching a graceful gazelle run free. Every corner of her existence is brimming with God's favor because she remained faithful through years in the fire. If people only knew that the great compassion she exudes on the job comes from a great place of pain and personal triumph.

I know it well. Because she is me, and I am her. This is why I celebrate my married friends. No, we're not mirror images. While we're on the phone, I have dogs jockeying for my attention, and she has toddlers doing the same. I have a host of interesting suitors, while she has a devoted husband. My evening routine has me in pajamas and in bed by nine. Her shut-eye doesn't come until midnight. I learn from the example of her life, this living, breathing, tangible dream I have long prayed for. She is proof that it can actually happen. And when it doesn't, I am proof that it is still a worthy life without the fulfillment of the dream.

∼೨

"A friend loves at all times,
and a [sister] is born for adversity."

PROVERBS *17:17*

∼೨

What lessons have your married friends taught you about the realities of marriage and family? How has being single influence your beliefs about marriage?

Too...

Once I was told that I was both intelligent and strategic, but I don't think the man who uttered those words meant it as a compliment. I wish I had twenty dollars for every time I was criticized for being too strong, too smart, or too assertive. Perhaps it's the reason I'm still single. Maybe. Maybe not.

It probably never occurred to him (or others) that I didn't have a choice. We are, after all, the sum total of our life experiences. I grew up in a single-parent home in public housing. My only image of a father was a faded Polaroid of a man hovered over my one-year old frame; my outstretched arms and hands were holding onto his fingers. You could see my face in the photo but not his. Fatherless humble beginnings laid the foundation for hard work and determination. Any strength I attained was the consequence of great fear. By the time I learned to be more vulnerable and less self-righteous and self-critical, I'd already discarded a laundry list of loves. Perhaps it's the reason I'm still single. Maybe. Maybe not.

If I've stood on the shoulders of the likes of Ida B. Wells, then I'm unapologetic. If I'm cut from the same cloth as Sojourner Truth, then so be it. If I walk in the footsteps of a Michelle Obama, then I'm hopeful that intelligence, strategy, and strength will be revered, not repelled. Until then, I'm waiting to be told that I'm loving, kind, and loyal. I'm also waiting for someone to pay my mortgage. Now that would be a serious compliment!

~∘

*"I will praise You, for I am fearfully and wonderfully made;
marvelous are your works, and that
my soul knows very well."*

PSALM 139:14

~∘

SINGLE SERVING

How have your relationships impacted your self-esteem? How can you use your faith to see yourself as God sees you?

U R Loved

She hadn't yet considered that the voice of the heart is the voice for God.

—MARIANNE WILLIAMSON

"You are loved." I've signed many letters, e-mails, and text messages with that phrase. It was my way of saying I love you to friends, family members, or a love interest, especially when I was afraid, embarrassed, or bracing for rejection. Bit by bit, singleness has taught me to be bold and courageous in love. I realized that there's nothing to lose by demonstrating great care, concern, and compassion for others. How can we expect great love if we can't freely express it? More importantly, how can we learn to give it without the expectation of anything in return?

I am love. It's a phrase I often repeat to myself. If we're willing, singleness can actually teach us selflessness in preparation for the right relationship. Just like our love for the Lord (and His love for us), it can't be contained, hidden from view, concealed, or rationed. It knows no bounds. It has no limits. It can free a slave. It can uplift the downtrodden. Not every encounter has to be the love of your life. But every encounter is an opportunity to show God's love.

~

"He who does not love does not know God, for God is love."

1 JOHN 4:8

~

How do you express God's love for others? How might you remind yourself that you are loved?

Imagine

Logic will get you from A to B. Imagination will take you everywhere.

As a child, I loved to play dress-up. I'd bang out soap-opera scripts or short stories on an old Smith Corona typewriter, and then act them out. To encourage my performances, my mother took me to the thrift store to find stage clothes for all of my characters. Once she bought me a long black wig that I boldly wore outside. My poor mother! How embarrassing it must've been to watch me prancing around like Diana Ross in our neighborhood. The truth is, as an adult, I still pretend—with a bit more discretion. I've learned that a childlike imagination can be helpful. It can make the meantime bearable—even fun!

I'm reminded of an encounter in the jewelry section of Target years ago. I saw it. So I bought it. I liked the way it gleamed in the light, and I liked the thought of what people would think when I wore it in public. More importantly, I liked how it made me feel. It made me look like someone's wife. It was a tiny piece of cut glass, a cheap cubic zirconia pretending to be a two-carat princess-cut diamond. It didn't matter to me that it wasn't real. For $19.99 plus tax, I found a priceless fairy tale, a temporary membership in a sorority that had repeatedly rejected me. Oh the joy as I admired my decorated ring finger! At last, someone thought enough of me (and the feeling was mutual) that we agreed to spend the rest of our lives together. As business partners, we made a pact to create something in the world together. Whether it was children, a house, careers, money, or flowers in the backyard, we would do it together.

When I wear my "engagement ring and wedding band," I busy myself around the house, cleaning, doing laundry, cooking, making phone calls, setting up meetings, putting out fires, and all the sorts of things domesticated and career women who authentically wear these rings do. I fall asleep with it on my finger, and it greets me in the morning. In those moments, I am someone's wife. I'm taken. I've been snagged by some lucky, handsome man with a plan. For $19.99, that's not bad at all. Yes, it's silly and laughable. No, it's not real, and it's only for pretend. But the feeling is priceless.

"For where your treasure is, there your heart will be also."

MATTHEW 6:21

SINGLE SERVING

How do you use fantasy or laughter during your single journey?

Soak in Solitude

M orning prayer is everything. It sets the tone for the day. When my eyes open and my feet hit the floor, I pull back my curtains, and out of my mouth comes praise.

"This is the day the Lord has made; let me rejoice and be glad in it," I declare, letting the light of a summer day or the calm of a winter morning into my bedroom and my heart. "Greater is He that is in me than He that is in the world. I am never forsaken or begging for bread. When my mother and father forsake me, the Lord shall take me up. When anxieties are great within me, it is Your joy that brings me consolation. The Lord is the strength of my life. Whom shall I fear?"

Those words have power. They settle into my bones and give birth to a positive attitude. It's a daily reminder that, come what may, I am His, and He is mine. Everything that happened yesterday and everything that's coming tomorrow is His. Those quiet moments before the stress of the day overtakes me are precious. What a blessing in the midst of empty mornings. It's a luxury really. Only the single (and childless) can take full advantage of this. Like a warm bath that never goes cold, the single person gets the option to soak in the solitude. With little time to spare, the dutiful wife and mother has to praise and pray while she's ushering her husband and children out the door in the morning. A moment to herself is a rare treasure. Of course, I'd trade in an empty morning for the frenzy of a family preparing for the day ahead. But oh! How I would miss that morning moment when my eyes open and it's just me and Him.

~⁀

*"In the morning, Lord, you hear my voice; in the morning
I lay my requests before you and wait expectantly."*

Psalm 5:3

~⁀

SINGLE SERVING

Do you pray in the morning? Commit yourself to a week or morning prayer. How might marriage change your daily routine? What is it about being single that you appreciate?

Love Something (or Someone)

Think of a time when you were moving or leaving good friends or a beloved family behind. Maybe you were headed off to college or moving to a new state to start a new job. You probably waved as you drove away or boarded your plane. But did you remember to leave a little love? That's exactly what Jesus did as he shared those last precious moments with his disciples.

If only we were always so brave as to speak and pour out an abundance of love. We're human. We qualify how and how much we're willing to give based on whether we'll get it back.

Hurt makes us hesitant.

History can put a halt to it.

Disappointment can dissuade us.

Differences can redirect it.

Anger can make us hold love hostage.

Consider this: it's really not yours to give. When genuine love is brimming in your spirit, it can hardly be contained. You can't hide it or disguise it. It is what it is—a manifestation of Him, the One who loved us first without question, without qualifiers, without a care for whether it would be returned. I recall an interview featuring Oprah, in which she said that when she makes charitable donations, she does so from a place of genuine love and no regard for how the person or group will use it. I'm paraphrasing, but she essentially said it was none of her business what the recipient of her generosity did with it. They could've used the cash as wallpaper. Regardless, her love went out into the world. She poured out without regard for the outcome.

As I mature, I'm no longer embarrassed by those three little words: I love you. They escape my lips (probably too often) as I consider how we never know when it'll be the last time we speak to someone. When dealing with an abrasive personality now, something grabs hold of me and I'm less inclined to meet ire with ire. I think of the most loving response that I can humanly muster in that moment.

It amazes me how fear, pride, insecurity, and self-righteousness can convince people to either withhold or resist love altogether. When Jesus said it was a new commandment, he never mentioned it had to meet a certain criterion. He just told those disciples to go out and give it, knowing that human weakness would be the greatest challenge to their charge. A dear friend of mine recently returned to online dating after a few dating disasters and disappointments. Determined not to give up, she declared over Sunday brunch, "You just gotta go out there and love something!"

That's the spirit! Now go out there, and pour it out.

"A new command I give you; Love one another.
As I have loved you, so you must love one another.
By this everyone will know that you are my disciples,
if you love one another."

J𝗈𝗁𝗇 *13:34–35*

SINGLE SERVING

How might you begin to show more courage in love with a potential spouse and others?

Eternal Sunshine

It was a dreary, overcast kind of day. The rain was coming down outside, but I was settled in at the counter of a little diner appropriately called the Eternal Sunshine Café. The waitress was sunny, and her blond curls were held back by a leopard-print bandana. The menu was eclectic and creative, with items like banana foster French toast and cinnamon-swirl pancakes. The older man who sat next to me scarfed down his omelet while scanning the local paper. Earlier, he'd desperately wanted to strike up a conversation. But I politely gave him social cues with a smile and brief answers to his questions. I was already too busy with the conversation in my head. I was on vacation from a high-demand job. I came there to rest, to think, to write, and to make an admission to myself and my heavenly Father.

I am afraid.

Every time I'm at a crossroad like this, I become fully aware of what it really means to be single. All roads begin and end with me. Just me. This is not to discount the sovereignty of God. But there are major decisions to be made, not by committee, but by an executive order in a party of one. On one hand, the autonomy is a beautiful blessing. There are no others to take into consideration. On the other hand, it's a stark reminder that there may never be others to take into consideration—no dinner-table family meetings or midnight pillow talk with my husband.

Next comes a heart-pounding question: will it *always* be this way? The thing that keeps even the most contented single woman up at night, anxious about the future, is whether she will grow old alone. Beyond the brave and seemingly unaffected face, it's good to admit this from time to time. I think God appreciates this brand of transparency. After all, He already knows when we wrestle with unbelief. It's good to admit when we see a little bit of ourselves in the old guy at the counter, trying to make eye contact with anyone willing to chat about the weather. He simply wants a connection, and it's painfully obvious.

In addition to the daily declaration of encouragement, the consistent ability to speak over yourself, to recite scripture, and to commit it to your heart, the single person's faith walk also requires honesty. Real honesty. It's a trusted friend on a rainy day, a little ray of sunshine, a single seat at a countertop café.

~∂

"And you will know the truth,
and the truth will set you free."

John 8:32

~∂

SINGLE SERVING

Take a moment to be really honest with yourself. How might your faith help you with uncomfortable truths?

Bucket List

A bucket list should include all of the things you hope to experience before the sunset of your life. Whether they're silly, adventurous, courageous, or even strange, it doesn't matter. It's your list. From European travel destinations to a Broadway musical stage performance, my list also includes some embarrassing things that I had hoped to experience as an engaged or married woman. Just once, I'd like to change my relationship status on social media to married and watch the congratulatory messages pour in. I'd like to visit upscale bridal boutiques and spend the day with girlfriends, trying on wedding dresses. I'd like to don a pair of cowboy boots and be photographed at an old farm with a dreamy bouquet in my hand.

Far less romantic and more rooted in reality is a line item I recently checked off the list. I had longed for a career change, but fear of the unknown (and a lucrative salary) kept me paralyzed for years. Where would I go? What else was I capable of doing? I had been a one-trick pony for twenty years. I thought I needed a husband, a supportive partner to make such a daring and bold transition. With someone by my side, I thought it would be easier. I thought there would be less of a chance of failure. And if I did, at least someone would be there to break my fall. What I've learned is this: there are no perfect plans; there's just God. We don't always know how things will work out. All we know is there's one constant, consistent player on our team. There's just a Father who loves us perfectly—win or lose. So after a long time of washing my nets like Simon, I finally stood up and stepped outside the boat. There was only one hand stretched out, waiting for me. Just as Peter did, I was determined to walk when Jesus called my name. An invitation to trust Him is walk-on-water faith. It allows for our greatest fears but also requires us to abandon doubt with every courageous step we take.

Don't wait for the perfect conditions. Just do it—whatever it is.

~⁀

"And He said, 'Come!' And Peter got out of the boat, and walked on the water and came toward Jesus. But seeing the wind, he became frightened, and beginning to sink, he cried out, 'Lord, save me!' Immediately Jesus stretched out His hand and took hold of him, and said to him, 'You of little faith, why did you doubt?'"

MATTHEW 14:29–31

~⁀

SINGLE SERVING

How might you demonstrate "walk-on-water faith" in the most challenging areas of your life? Create a prayer you can recite when you need it.

Blessing of the Moment

I f only the view from my yoga mat could be like this every day. The waves crashing, a gentle breeze, and the occasional squawking of a bird lulled me into a deep meditative state. I stared out into the vast openness. There was only a lone parasurfer, jumping from crest to crest on his board with a sturdy hand on his kite. I didn't even notice how close the bird was standing next to me. However, I was startled when the water threatened to overtake my mat. I leaped to my feet and quickly grabbed the rubber foam before it was whisked away. It was an indication that I had been sitting for a long while, just looking out, breathing, and thinking.

Perhaps the only downside to singleness is the open invitation to think. Thinking about the past. Thinking about the future. Thinking about the would've, could've, and should've. Wondering how the story will unfold. Will I get my happily ever after? Introspection is good, but too much can also be a burden, a thief of peace. There can be an overconsumption of oneself. It can block out the blessing of the moment, the wisdom in unexpected places.

There on my mat, with the Atlantic Ocean as my personal studio, I was greeted by a stranger. He was with his wife, taking a casual stroll in front of me. He waved, and I politely responded with the same. His wife started to tell me a story about her encounter with the fearless bird that was still holding its post next to me. She had made the mistake of feeding it, which attracted a dozen of its flying friends. I smiled and laughed at her story, wishing they'd move on so that I could get back to meditating and praying—in peace.

The man told me he had seen me doing yoga earlier. He'd been practicing mindfulness meditation to clear his mind. Trying not to show my agitation, I patiently entertained his comments and questions. *Move along*, I thought. Then he dropped a pearl like an oyster right out of the ocean behind us.

"You know, the goal is not peace," he said with a thick Southern accent. "The goal is awareness. Through awareness, you find peace."

As if he'd known me my entire single life, he encouraged me to clear my mind of the past and avoid fruitless worry about the future. They moseyed along after that, walking hand in hand down the shore. I was stunned. God is always watching. He knows the burden of all our thoughts. I took a deep breath and forced all five of my senses to take note of everything in that moment.

~

"Be still, and know that I am God."

PSALM 46:10

~

SINGLE SERVING

While you wait, how do you remain faithful in the present and avoid thoughts about the past and future?

God Says No

What if God says no? I know it's an uncomfortable outcome. It goes against everything we've been taught about steadfast prayer, walking in faith, and believing without sight. What if He says no to what you've been asking for all this time? I bravely posed the question in a journal entry. I've kept a diary since I was in the fourth grade. This time, I asked God if marriage and motherhood was my assignment, or if singleness was my ministry. Though my heart ached for the former, years later, the answer was revealed to be the latter.

I guess it's why I pay close attention to love, especially among older couples. I encounter five senior couples on my early-morning power walk in my neighborhood. I adore them. I want to be them. I need to see them as I push through. They're well beyond retirement, living out their days and managing physical ailments together. They're like a rainbow of seasoned love: Asian, Black, White, Indian, and Hispanic. One of the wives with a hip injury hobbles behind her husband while the others walk alongside their beloveds. Some hold hands while others forge ahead together, yet with a spirit of independence. If I'm honest, I've run ahead of a few men in my past. It wasn't out of arrogance or stubborn resistance to being led. No, it was because I'm captivated, maybe even driven, by my own power and need for accomplishment. That's not a bad thing in the absence of a hunter and a gatherer, because it's kept food on my table. It does, however, increase the risk of running solo. Fearless, fierce, and free aren't always attributes appreciated by every man—even those who claim they want an equal.

Maybe there are only so many Baracks for the Michelles. Maybe someone peering out the window in the early morning needs to see me. Me, living out my single-digit equation. Me, powering through without a helpmate. Just me, faithful in my singleness. God still has use for the legions of women just like me.

By the way, I recently saw the couple with the wife nursing a hip injury. On that particular morning, she hobbled ahead, while her devoted husband patiently followed from behind. I needed to see that.

~

"For still the vision awaits its appointed time; it hastens to the end—it will not lie. If it seems slow, wait for it; it will surely come; it will not delay."

HABAKKUK 2:3

~

SINGLE SERVING

How has being single strengthened your commitment to your faith and made you a better believer?

Choose Joy

The joy of the Lord can ease any emotional and physical pain and bring you a new level of satisfaction in life.

—JOYCE MEYER

The subconscious is a powerful tool. Think of how an elementary classroom is decorated with bright colors and words of encouragement. Every morning, a sign in the kitchen greets me. When I walk down the hallway, I consciously read the words, "I choose joy!" Day after day, it's embedded in my brain. That's the goal. Those words are scribbled in chalk on a blackboard, along with a quote, a line from a song, or a piece of scripture meant to motivate me. All of it is deposited in my subconscious mind. I always carry it with me because we cannot control every detail of our circumstances, but we do have a choice in how we respond to it.

We're designed for partnership, especially women. That yearning at your core is as it should be—the way God intended. Until it's fulfilled, don't waste time denying it and pretending as though it doesn't matter. Honor it by choosing joy. Consciously choose joy, because disappointment is a soul-sucking spirit-drainer. Besides, "choose disappointment" on a chalkboard just doesn't seem right.

~⁹

"You make known to me the path of life; in your presence there is fullness of joy; at your right hand are pleasures forevermore."

PSALM 16:11

~⁹

SINGLE SERVING

In what ways do you choose joy? How do you think happiness differs from joy? How might your remind yourself to choose joy each day?

Love Later in Life

After a certain age, there are two possible outcomes: you are destined to be fabulously single, or you are destined for love later in life. Whenever I think of the latter, a lovely couple in their sixties comes to mind. I remember how sweet they were together at a friend's dinner party. The wife is a dessert chef, and the cake she brought to the gathering was divine. But it was her husband's reaction to the fondant that stuck with me.

Clearly, he loved helping her in the kitchen. I listened as he anxiously watched us sampling the cake. He wondered if he hadn't executed the icing to her liking. She quickly dismissed his disappointment and reassured him that his work was perfect, just like he was. She communicated this with a touch of her hand, a softness in her voice, and a tilt of her head near his shoulder. He beamed with pride, as if he'd just changed the carburetor in their car or custom-built shelves in their garage. It was both Herculean and adorable. Here was a man in love, not only taking an interest in what brought his best friend joy but also actively participating in it. If that's love later in life, I'll wait for my slice at sixty, seventy, or even eighty.

"But if we hope for what we do not see,
we wait for it with patience."

ROMANS 8:25

SINGLE SERVING

How long are you willing to wait for your heart's desire? What if it takes years to come to pass?

The Great Love

The Great Love. Perhaps there are no sweeter words.
Put this book down, and put your hand over your heart, and say it again and again and again. Lift that prayer to the heavens.

The Great Love.

Think about it: the ultimate sacrifice came from a single man. His name is Jesus.

Tears well up in my eyes when I think of the Garden of Gethsemane. Jesus asked for the support of his disciples, who, in their understandable weariness, fell asleep and left him alone. There, in the dark of the night, as terror gripped him, it was just Jesus. His fear and his desperation were his only companions. That was it. No one except death was coming. Without the comfort of another to lean on or cheer him on, Jesus courageously accepted his assignment. He took the only hand available to him in the moment. He knew he was made for love.

"Please take this cup of suffering away from me," he whispers to his Abba Father, already knowing the answer. "Yet I want your will to be done, not mine."

With that, the ultimate sacrifice beyond comprehension came from a single person. Can we accept our assignments, knowing that in the absence of a covenant with another—maybe even in the absence of children—we are still made for love? The Great Love needs our sacrifice too.

Months after I went through a bad breakup, a dear friend asked me to write a letter on behalf of her husband, who was seeking citizenship in the United States. She asked me to be a witness, to attest to their love. How easy it would've been to tell her no in an act of selfish rebellion. Instead, I put pen to paper and told the attorney that their new marriage was "an enviable union that would suffer greatly if they were ever apart. Prayerfully, this beloved couple will have the chance to continue to live out their love story."

I wrote that knowing that a few years before, when she had first told me about him, I also had that same hope for a love story of my own. But His will, not mine. My letter, while not a march to a crucifixion, was a small sacrifice as I nursed a broken heart. The last thing I wanted to do was stand up for love, but how could I not when I was made for it?

Time and time again, I would be called to be a witness. When I was a reluctant bridesmaid, a dear friend asked me to recite the poem "Blessing of the Hands" at her wedding. The single, unmarried, and unlucky-in-love friend was asked to bless their union with the spoken word. How could that be? But I looked out into the crowd and proudly stood at the altar where the priest had made a declaration just moments before. The lovers looked deep into each other's eyes, yet were still fully aware that I was there with them. They wanted me there. I was made for love.

It was love when I rushed to the hospital one summer afternoon after a dear friend delivered her firstborn. He was perfect and beautiful. This is how hospital scenes should play out, I thought. Then she asked me to clothe his tiny body in his first little outfit, a ritual usually reserved for new mothers. When she learned she was expecting twins a few years later, I was among the first she called to share the good news.

"You have such a love for children," she said.

Yes, I do. I was made for love. So when a couple that I'm friends with asked me to be their daughter's custodial parent in a living will in the event that they should die, I lovingly agreed. The single friend with no children is whom they wanted to entrust with their baby girl's future. How could this be? The only explanation is that I was made for love.

With or without a husband, you are made for love. The Great Love has designed you for that purpose. Your covenant with the people in your life is just as valuable as a union with only one. Never stop being a walking, living, breathing manifestation of His love. Don't you know that you are a character in the greatest love story ever told? Now, bravely walk in it. After all, you already know how the ending goes.

～౨

*"There's no greater love than to
lay down one's life for one's friends."*

JOHN 15:13

～౨

SINGLE SERVING

How does your faith and devotion as a single person inspire others? How do you demonstrate love to family, friends, coworkers, and even your enemies?

Additional Servings

Of Strength
Colossians 3:2
Psalm 18:2
2 Kings 6:16–17
Zephaniah 3:17

Of Motivation
Colossians 3:23
Habakkuk 3:19
1 John 4:19
2 Chronicles 15:7

Of Affirmation
1 Corinthians 2:9
Psalm 23:1
Proverbs 3:5
Ephesians 6:13

Of Courage
1 John 4:4
Proverbs 28:1
Psalm 16:11
Proverbs 18:10

Of Armor
Ephesians 6:10–18
James 1:12
Romans 8:37
Proverbs 15:13–14

Of Self-Love
Romans 8:31
Hebrews 10:35
Corinthians 13:
James 4:6

Of Positivity
Romans 12:12
3 John 1:2
Proverbs 4:23
Proverbs 19:8

Of Growth
1 Corinthians 3:6–9
Colossians 3:17 2
Psalm 139:14
Matthew 6:28–29 1

Of Joy
Lamentations 3:22–23
Corinthians 12:10
Psalm 37:4
Corinthians 13:11

Of Friendship
1 Thessalonians 5:11
Proverbs 27:17
Matthew 7:3
Deuteronomy 31:6

Of Perseverance
Hebrews 10:35–36
Philippians 1:6
Psalm 57:12
Ephesians 4:32

Of Faith
Matthew 14:22–23
Psalm 121
Joshua 1:9
Psalm 26:2–3

Tamara B. Gibbs

Tamara Gibbs is the founder and creator of Single Serving for Single Women, a Christian digital ministry targeting single women. Born out of her desire to encourage herself, Single Serving for Single Women offers original, visually engaging daily inspirational quotes to its growing fan base on social media. The digital ministry serves up #MorningPrayer tweets and scripture along with a weekly blog series. In *Single Serving for Single Women: A Fifty Day Devotional*, Tamara B. Gibbs is willing to walk in faith with her readers.

The Emmy-nominated journalist turned author defines herself as a believer, speaker, writer, and teacher. After sixteen years as a broadcast journalist in the Raleigh-Durham market, Tamara is a familiar face in Central North Carolina. She traded in her reporter notepad and pen in pursuit of a change in pace and the chance to speak and write aloud for God.

In addition to serving as a public relations professional, she is an adjunct professor and the coproducer of an upcoming documentary entitled Victims of Faith, produced by Front Runner Productions. The feature film will explore the role of faith in the fatal shooting of three Muslim students in Chapel Hill, North Carolina.

Made in the USA
San Bernardino, CA
18 October 2016